PREFACE

THE LATER seventeenth century is perhaps the first moment in British history that we can truly hear people talking. For earlier periods, our knowledge of their dialogue comes through the ears and pens of poets like Chaucer, or playwrights like Shakespeare. But now, for the first time, we can hear their own voices, un-moderated, in their diaries, in the journals of their travels, or in journalism. Samuel Pepys, John Evelyn, Daniel Defoe, Celia Fiennes, John Bunyan – all of them great writers, with a great eye for the land and the times they lived in, and with a direct, unaffected style that speaks straight to us. We also know something of the characters of the day – not just the highborn, but some of the more ordinary folk who attracted attention: people like the courtesan Nell Gwyn or (very different in almost every respect) the founder of the Quakers, George Fox – himself another indefatigable diarist. For this reason, this period is perhaps the first one that seems close to us, a time we could imagine inhabiting – especially as we also see this as the beginning of the consumer culture that began really to thrive in the Georgian era. Yet the Great Fire, and the Plague, events so vividly described by the diarists, remind us how much more dangerous life was even then.

In this volume we have tried to outline the realities of life, how people behaved, what the towns and houses felt like and smelt like. We have also tried to show what it looked like. Most of the paintings of the period showed aristocrats in their finery – but this was a time when the influence of Holland was strong in England, and the Dutch painters were fascinated by the minutiae of everyday life. Many of these paintings finished up in England – and we have drawn on these, as well as the range of other visual matter, to get as close as we can to the real living history of Restoration England.

Peter Furtado
General Editor

Opposite:
One of the Henrician castles on the Kentish coast at the heart of English naval control over the Channel; England's growing dominance of the sea, for trade and politics, came to affect the lives of ever more people during the Restoration period.

RESTORATION
ENGLAND

1660–1699

Peter Furtado

SHIRE LIVING HISTORIES

How we worked • How we played • How we lived

Published in Great Britain in 2010 by Shire Publications
Ltd, Midland House, West Way, Botley, Oxford OX2 0PH,
United Kingdom.

44-02 23rd Street, Suite 219, Long Island City, NY 11101,
USA.

E-mail: shire@shirebooks.co.uk   www.shirebooks.co.uk

© 2010 Shire Publications.

Every attempt has been made by the Publishers to secure
the appropriate permissions for materials reproduced in
this book. If there has been any oversight we will be happy
to rectify the situation and a written submission should be
made to the Publishers.

A CIP catalogue record for this book is available from the
British Library.

Shire Living Histories No. 6   ISBN-13: 978 0 74780 793 3

Peter Furtado has asserted his right under the Copyright,
Designs and Patents Act, 1988, to be identified as the
author of this book.

Designed by Myriam Bell Design, France, and typeset in
Perpetua and Janson Text.

Printed in China through Worldprint Ltd.

10 11 12 13 14   10 9 8 7 6 5 4 3 2 1

COVER IMAGE
Coffee house c.1700. (Granger Collection/Topfoto.)

PHOTOGRAPH ACKNOWLEDGEMENTS
Akg-images, pages 53, 54; Ambrett, page 43; Bridgeman
Art Library: Bonhams, London, pages 21, 22, Christie's
Images, pages 30, 47, Detroit Institute of Arts, USA, page
42, Ferens Art Gallery, Hull City Museums and Art
Galleries, page 40, Fitzwilliam Museum, Cambridge,
pages 14 (right), 15, Guildhall Art Gallery, City of
London, page 16 (top), Manchester Art Gallery, page 31,
Noortman Master Paintings, Amsterdam, page 36, Victoria
& Albert Museum, London, page 23, private collections,
pages 16 (bottom), 32, 39, 41 (top), 48; British Library,
pages 20 (bottom), 24 (top); Steve Cadnam, page 20 (top);
Corbis, pages 6, 77 (bottom); English Heritage, pages 4,
12, 18, 26–7, 46 (bottom), 62, 72; Getty Images,
pages 31 (bottom), 68; Museum of London, pages 8 (top),
44 (bottom); National Maritime Museum, page 38
(bottom); Shire Publications, by Graham Turner, pages
64–5; Pete Reed, page 25; Sue Ross, page 51; Topfoto,
pages 11, 14 (left), 28, 33 (right), 41 (bottom), 58 (right),
60, 61, 66, 69 (top), 70 (top), 71, 75 (top), 78.

All other images are from the author's collection.

Shire Publications is supporting the Woodland Trust, the UK's leading woodland conservation charity, by funding the dedication of trees.

CONTENTS

INTRODUCTION

THE PEOPLE of Dover waved and cheered on 25 May 1660 when Charles II, his pet dog tucked under his arm, stepped ashore from his exile in Holland. Oliver Cromwell's republic was finally over, a year after the death of its founder. The following April, Londoners cheered when Charles was crowned King of England, France and Ireland, King of Scots, and Defender of the Faith (no-one really believed he was king of France; this was an old title dating from the time of the Hundred Years War). Back with the King came theatres, games and Christmas, all of them banned over the previous decade. It was as if the extremists, the religious radicals who wanted to tell people how they should live and what they could and couldn't think and do, had been finally defeated. Life was back to normal.

But what was normality? It is true that the violence that had raged up and down the land in the civil wars of the 1640s was not repeated – apart from one bloody battle at Sedgemoor in 1685, when the Duke of Monmouth's scratch army of Somerset yeomen was cut to pieces by James II's army. Ordinary people were no longer in immediate physical danger from the high politics of the realm as they had been when the king and parliament were at war with one another. Affairs of state were still tense, however, and military force was sometimes used – as when William of Orange brought an army of Dutchmen to drive James II off the throne in 1688 (it didn't actually need to fight as James's commander John Churchill went over to William's side), and when the two fought a pitched battle on the River Boyne in Ireland two years later. But, for the most part, the ordinary people of England, Wales and Scotland could again go about their business without fear that an army might march through their towns, turn them out of their homes or trample their crops. One of the promises that William of Orange made when he became king as William III was that there would be no more large 'standing' armies kept in Britain in peacetime.

Opposite:
This was an age of scientific advance, as many scholars and men of letters took an interest in what was called 'natural philosophy'. Isaac Newton was the most famous scientist of the period, for his work on optics, astronomy, mathematics and gravity. This image shows his telescope.

7

The coronation procession of the restored King Charles II, on 23 April 1661, was an occasion for general rejoicing. His regime remained popular, at least until he was suspected of conversion to Catholicism and of supporting the authoritarian and Catholic Louis XIV of France.

Nor were people any longer in serious danger of dying as a result of their religious beliefs. Not that it was a tolerant age, in this respect at least. It certainly was not easy to disagree with the orthodoxies of the Church of England: you might find yourself hounded by your neighbours, flung into jail, refused an education and unable to find a job, but it generally wasn't actually life-threatening. The old arguments about theology – the details of the Christian faith and what church services meant – had mostly turned into arguments about loyalty to England, the English people and their traditional way of life. Catholics, who were loyal to the pope in Rome, were feared as traitors who might let a tyrannical king of France take away the freedoms of ordinary people – and the suspicion that Charles II might be a closet Catholic, and the certainty that James II was a shameless one, were seen as political threats to the rights of ordinary Englishmen.

At the other end of the religious and political spectrum were religious radicals like Quakers who believed that everyone was equal before God; this, and their insistence on expressing the belief in their language, clothing and everyday behaviour, meant they were thought to be dangerous revolutionaries who were upsetting the new stability

The staircase in the monument built in the 1670s close to Pudding Lane where the Fire of London began. Its inscription reads, in part, 'London rises again, whether with greater speed or greater magnificence is doubtful, three short years complete that which was considered the work of an age'.

of the social order. But those who did not argue with most of what the clergyman preached in the pulpit of their parish church need not worry too much about exactly what they believed, and could get on with the business of living in peace: building up their wealth, and making themselves and their homes more comfortable than ever before. The men enjoyed gossiping and sipping hot drinks in coffee houses, while the women looked after them and faced a barrage of sexual advances with robust good humour.

A woodcut of St Paul's Cathedral in flames, for many the most grievous aspect of the Great Fire of London, 1666.

Such, at least, is the picture of life which we get from some of the most famous diary writers in English history, especially Samuel Pepys who wrote coded accounts of his daily doings through most of the 1660s and left a uniquely rich picture of the life and secret thoughts of a busy and prosperous middle-class man in Restoration London. When today we read Pepys as he writes about what he has just had for lunch, how he is worrying about his health, the jollity of Christmas at home, how he makes passes at the servants of his friends and what happens when his wife finds out, we feel we are eavesdropping on someone we know and are right there with him in his house on Seething Lane near the Tower of London. Above all we feel that the life this ambitious civil servant was leading was a normal one, a life we can easily recognise and identify with.

Although it feels familiar to us in some respects, Pepys's world was quite different from our own, and it was also very different from the world that Shakespeare had lived in, little more than fifty years before. The Plague of 1665, the Great Fire of London of 1666, both of which Pepys described with heartbreaking immediacy, remind us how much more fragile – and short – life was then than now. His wife Elizabeth was just fifteen when they married, and she died of typhoid at only twenty-nine. This was not at all unusual. Yet in other ways England was more stable than in Shakespeare's day: where once bands

Part of the very first entry of Pepys's diary, 1 January 1660, showing the shorthand that protected his innermost thoughts from prying eyes. It says: 'The condition of the State was thus. Viz. the Rump, after being disturbed by my Lord Lambert, was lately returned to sit again. The officers of the army all forced to yield. Lawson lie[s] still in the River and Monke is with his army in Scotland.'

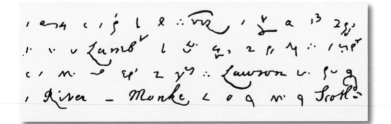

of paupers had roamed the land, thrown into poverty by an increasing population, rising prices, and new methods of farming, now the growing population – there were probably about 6 million people in Great Britain in 1700 – was no longer causing widespread poverty but was accompanied by a steady rise in prosperity. The first signs of commercial sophistication and industrial development were visible, the beginnings of consumerism were evident and England was slowly beginning to turn into what Napoleon – a hundred years later – was to call 'a nation of shopkeepers'.

Though Charles Stuart had resolved 'never to go on his travels again', his youthful years in exile in France and Holland had shaped him, and meant that the society of his court was a more cosmopolitan one than England had known for several centuries. The 'Glorious Revolution' of 1688 brought a substantial number of Dutchmen with William of Orange and put them close to the heart of the nation's affairs, while the new policy of engagement in war with France also served to bring England ever closer to the continent. Some Dutch artists came to work in Britain; others remained in Holland but their paintings graced the walls of English homes, often showing scenes of everyday life in the Low Countries.

Far from the capital, life was changing much more slowly, and for the Scots it was especially different from life in Pepys's London. Scotland still had its own crown (even though its king was also the

Hampton Court Palace saw a major extension for William and Mary. It was built by Christopher Wren in an imposing style that, typically for its age, used brick rather than stone.

king of England), its own church and its own parliament; economic change was slow to start and the Scots were beginning to feel like the poor relations of the English. Ever since the Civil War, people both rich and poor had travelled back and forth across the border in increasing numbers, and now the idea of creating a united kingdom of England, Wales and Scotland was talked about for the first time. Whether this would relieve the poverty that brought terrible famines for much of the 1690s and killed perhaps one in ten of the Scottish people, nobody knew for sure.

The Battle of Sedgemoor, 6 July 1685, the last battle to date to be fought on English soil, saw the forces of the usurping Duke of Monmouth destroyed by those of James II, commanded by John Churchill, later Duke of Marlborough.

On the following pages we shall look at the realities of life – and death – in the later seventeenth century. While Pepys will help us see how people lived, we shall travel more widely than he did, both up and down the social scale and across the realm, to find out what really was normal for people in the later Stuart years, and how it relates to what we call normal today. We shall look at the paintings of the Dutch genre painters, the political broadsides, the books of household advice, the moralising sermons and much more to make life in late seventeenth-century England real again.

William of Orange, William III (r. 1689–1702), brought a flood of Dutch followers and Dutch style into Britain.

FAMILY

THE 'MERRY MONARCH' Charles II had his string of mistresses, from aristocratic Lady Castlemaine to the orange-seller Nell Gwyn, and Samuel Pepys was unable to meet a pretty woman – be she wife of a colleague, daughter of a neighbour or his own household servant – without his hands wandering. We think of the Restoration years as a time of physical pleasure, at least for the young and healthy, who were far less fettered by the constraints of conscience, or fear of the flames of hell, than previous generations. So much so that by the 1690s a wave of sermons and moralising books condemned the 'vice' of the day – but probably without great effect.

Yet death was always just around the corner and not just during the devastating outbreak of plague; smallpox was a continual killer in the towns, while increasing overseas travel was bringing in some new diseases: malaria (which was then called 'ague') could be found in the marshes of the Thames Estuary. Children were the most vulnerable to sickness, especially in the cities: in London half of all deaths were of children under the age of ten, and a woman might have six or seven pregnancies: some had far more – between 1684 and 1700, for example, the future Queen Anne had seventeen pregnancies, but only one child survived infancy and even he died aged eleven.

So, though life expectancy overall was far lower than it is today, anyone who made it to adulthood could hope to live to around sixty. As people arrived at adulthood, they planned for marriage and family in a manner quite familiar to us, juggling romantic, financial, social and logistical considerations in varying proportions depending on circumstances and world-view.

Marriage was a market in which people looked for the best catch they could get; but most people – except the wealthiest – also probably married for love; a writer in 1696 said a happy marriage required 'virtuous inclinations, hearty love and true liking, so that they may both be of the same mind and have one and the same

Opposite:
A wedding by the Dutch artist Jan Steen, painted in 1667. He never visited England, but equivalent English peasant nuptials were probably similarly riotous and casual.

interest.' Theoretically a girl could marry at twelve, and a boy at fourteen; but people tended to wait until they were in a position to set up a household of their own, which usually meant their middle or later twenties. The favourite times of year for a wedding were late spring, after the annual lambing or calving, and late autumn, after the harvest. But those who needed a secret, quick or cheap marriage – or who didn't want the traditional banns to be read – could get one by hiring a priest to perform a private ceremony in the upstairs room of an inn, or in the chapel of London's Fleet Prison.

Once they were wed, the man was the master, responsible for all major decisions; his needs were always paramount, his opinions like unchallengeable laws within the household. One writer explained, 'every family must have its proper superior whom all the rest must needs obey.' As soon as she was married, everything a woman owned became the property of her husband (although he could not sell it without her permission). Her rights in law were very limited: were she to kill her husband, she could be tried not just for murder but for treason, and if convicted she would be burned alive. Divorce was virtually impossible, but men, in particular, might desert the marriage and leave their wife destitute. And it was not unknown (though it was in fact illegal) for men who were tired of their wives to take them to market with a halter round their necks and sell them to the highest bidder.

Whatever the legal rights and wrongs, a woman had ways of getting what she wanted out of her husband. If she found out about it, Elizabeth Pepys was capable of ending Samuel's

errant behaviour for a while. She was also capable of making her own choices, such as to take dancing lessons and then fall for her teacher (thereby arousing her husband's jealousy). Although a wife was not supposed to go into business herself, or even sell any property without her husband's consent, she might well assist her husband in his trade. As housekeeper she had to manage the household finances, negotiate with tradesmen and often juggle to make ends meet. She also took on responsibility for the servants – looking after their emotional and spiritual well-being as well as ensuring that they did their jobs effectively – and caring for the children. She could decide how to spend her time, and was under few restrictions on going out alone. Should her husband die before her, she inherited a third of his estate, and could keep it in her own name. Some widows went into business in their own right, taking up trades such as printing.

This Delft plate of 1677 in the Dutch style shows the Queen with a servant helping her on with her shoes, plus a courtier and a knight in armour.

Many babies born in the towns, particularly to better-off parents, were sent off to wet-nurses in the country. This was thought to be better for the child's health than being brought up in the dirty town – but standards of care were variable, and it was not unknown for nurses accidentally to kill the child and try to hide the evidence. Until weaned at around twelve months of age, a baby was kept swaddled, or wrapped tightly, a practice that was thought to strengthen the bones. Once they began to walk, both boys and girls were dressed in a long gown called 'coats'. Common toys included rattles, whistles and dolls, which could be bought from street traders. From the age of three or four, children were introduced to the basic teachings of the Bible.

Historians once thought that because so many children died in their first years, parents could have had little affection for them. But the diaries of the time tell a different story: John Evelyn wrote of 'our extreme sorrow' when describing the death of one child, just a few weeks old; and of 'our inexpressible grief and affliction' on another bereavement, this time of a five-year-old son. A Frenchman reported disapprovingly that the English 'have extraordinary regard for young children, always flattering, always caressing, always applauding what they do'.

The Hales family, painted by the court artist Peter Lely as an aristocratic family wished to be seen: sober, dignified and classical.

This was a time when the first childcare manuals were written, and different approaches to childcare were discussed. Some of the greatest thinkers of the day got involved. Philosopher John Locke, for example, disapproved of swaddling, thought a child should not eat meat until the age of three, and was worried that too much cosseting would spoil a child, though beating could be counter-productive if done to excess.

From about the age of five, a child was expected to help in the house or assist the parents at their work; in many ways seen as a small adult. From fourteen, many children were sent away from home to work as servants or as apprentices for a term of seven years. During that time, the apprentice lived in the master's household, rarely if ever returning home, and subject to what could be a strict regime of hard work, strict discipline (including frequent beatings), poor food and no pay while they learned their trade. It is perhaps not surprising that apprentices had the reputation of getting together in gangs and running wild at times. A young person reached the age of legal responsibility at sixteen, and full adulthood at twenty-one.

Once a young couple was independent enough to court, the proper method was for the man to call on the girl at her house,

This image of a harvest supper may be a more realistic picture of the times, an opportunity for general merriment in this generally rather unbuttoned age.

and ask permission to step out together. They could enjoy each other's company freely in public, before finally – and with the girl's father's permission – becoming formally betrothed. Financial negotiation – on the dowry the bride would bring, and on the proportion of the property that would fall to her when her husband died – might take months to conclude before the families finally agreed to the wedding taking place. Usually people avoided having sex before marriage, but after betrothal a couple might be permitted to 'bundle', which meant heavy petting but with a chaperone nearby, or perhaps a board down the middle of the bed to keep the lovers from getting too close.

The quality of life for older people naturally depended on whatever resources they had built up in previous decades. A widow remarried if she could (and if she did, she was allowed to retain whatever property she had inherited from her first husband), but for those who were unable to, poverty frequently beckoned. Some lived in their children's households (though elderly married couples did so only rarely). Those unable to care for themselves were reduced to seeking refuge in an almshouse or hospital. In theory, old people were respected for their knowledge and wisdom, but in practice, the rise of book-learning among younger generations meant that the value of a lifetime's accumulated experience was much less respected.

Sobriety was the hallmark of the Quakers. They dressed modestly and refused to doff their caps to anyone, even the King, and were outlawed for their pains. This image shows William Penn, founder of the colony of Pennsylvania.

A man and his wife, with the kind of affection visible that can so often be found in the letters and diaries of the day.

17

HOME AND NEIGHBOURHOOD

A FTER THE GREAT FIRE of 1666 had destroyed around four-fifths of the property in the City, London had a unique opportunity to rebuild virtually the entire area of the old capital (the fire died down before it could reach the newer suburbs such as Covent Garden). Some of England's other cities suffered similar disasters and had similar opportunities to renew themselves: Warwick for example suffered grievously in 1694, and the following year the vast, rambling royal Palace of Whitehall also burned to the ground, leaving just a few remnants of its former glory, such as Inigo Jones's Banqueting House. But most towns remained a jumble of old and new, with continual building and rebuilding, and older properties adapted to new uses. The streets were still mostly narrow, filthy and very dark at night, the timber-framed houses looming over the noisy roads and overhanging the maze of courts and alleys where the poorer homes and workshops were congregated. Workshops, stables and shops, boarding houses and inns intermingled, and every day stinking night-soil carts rolled by, collecting ordure from the cesspits to be taken to the outskirts where it was dumped. Going in the other direction were carts laden with barrels of more or less fresh water for household use; piped water was available only to the very richest.

A few wider streets, especially those close to the market, cathedral or centre, were lined with grand houses for the nobility, churchmen, rich merchants and officers of the city itself and its wealthy guilds. After the Fire, Christopher Wren and others had tried to devise a new, less haphazard plan for London, but ownership disputes and the need to rebuild quickly made these impossible to realise. Despite this failure, building regulations were introduced: a maximum height – depending on whether the house fronted a main street (where four storeys plus cellar and garret were permitted, and which might have cost £400 to build) or a by-lane (two storeys); overhanging the foundation line was forbidden, and brick, or occasionally stone, was the required building material.

Opposite: Jan Steen's satirical *Dissolute Household* (mid-1660s) shows slovenliness, sloth and seduction, as well as animals and servants getting out of hand.

Right:
Bedford Row,
London, has a
terrace of houses
built by Nicholas
Barbon in the
1670s.

Below:
The Surrey house
where diarist
John Evelyn grew
up and where he
lived for the last
ten years of his
life. He began
writing his diary
as a teenager. His
other great life-
long passion, for
gardening, also
began when he
was a young man.

For new housing, flammable thatched roofs were banned – no thatched building was erected in London again until 1997 when the replica Globe Theatre was opened. Houses in the new style were erected in the London suburbs such as Bloomsbury and Soho, which were built by the speculator Nicholas Barbon. Barbon was also the inventor of fire insurance, and as such promoted his building speculations by determining that insurance premiums for timber-and-thatch buildings were double the rate paid by their neighbours with the new brick-and-tile homes. None of the domestic buildings put up in London in the wake of the Fire have survived; but the new fashion for brick houses, with distinctive large sash windows was taken up elsewhere in the country and can be seen in many smaller towns.

Most town houses, new or old, had a quite a large number of relatively small rooms, often brightened with decorated cloth or paper nailed to the wall. There was for the first time commonly a separate dining room, and many people took pride in their silver tableware, best decorated pottery and glass. Furniture was becoming more comfortable than ever before, with upholstered chairs and settees more common, often in bright and contrasting colours, and the first printed fabric patterns were available. Some houses had oak or, more often, pine panelling, often with classical designs, and the fireplace formed an elaborately decorated centrepiece, perhaps surrounded by blue-and-white Delft tiles and topped by a mirror. Rugs and carpets might be placed over bare polished floorboards. Metal 'branches' or candle-holders attached to the walls provided light.

An elegant walnut upholstered and cane-back chair of about 1680.

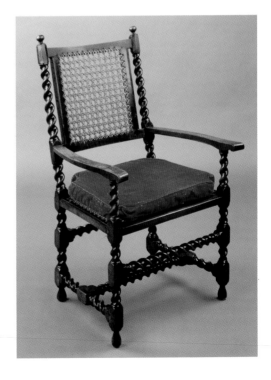

The most popular style of the period owed much to the two continental centres of France – though the English taste simplified much of the highly ornate decoration popular in Versailles – and Holland, where a new style more suitable for the wealthy town houses of merchants had developed mid-century. In the years following the Restoration, the order of

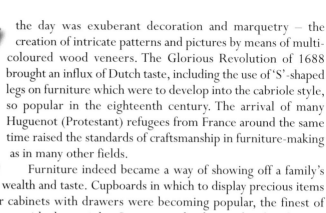

the day was exuberant decoration and marquetry – the creation of intricate patterns and pictures by means of multi-coloured wood veneers. The Glorious Revolution of 1688 brought an influx of Dutch taste, including the use of 'S'-shaped legs on furniture which were to develop into the cabriole style, so popular in the eighteenth century. The arrival of many Huguenot (Protestant) refugees from France around the same time raised the standards of craftsmanship in furniture-making as in many other fields.

Furniture indeed became a way of showing off a family's wealth and taste. Cupboards in which to display precious items or cabinets with drawers were becoming popular, the finest of them with elegant inlay. So too were bookcases, lined with gold-tooled leather spines. Wealthier householders also liked to display musical instruments such as viols or virginals, though racier households might have card tables instead. The improving quality of postal services was making letter-writing more popular, and one new item of fashionable furniture was the scriptor, writing desk or bureau; while another newly popular item of furniture was the long-case clock, which had been made possible by the invention of a new form of pendulum control in Holland in the 1650s. Very fine examples made by the top craftsmen in London, such as Thomas Tompion, displayed precision engineering in their movements, and magnificent craftsmanship in their decoration, but others, much cheaper but often still highly presentable, were made in provincial 'country' workshops by artisans. Indeed, the decades following 1680 are considered a golden age of English clockmaking.

The main bedroom would be dominated by a large bed, with mattresses of wool, straw and feather and hung with curtains that were often embroidered by the lady of the house. High chests of drawers were coming into use, replacing top-opening chests for storing clothes, and more elegant bedrooms might contain a dressing table with a mirror. A larger press (cupboard) was needed for the family's linen. To keep out the draughts, the windows were hung with heavy curtains, and shutters might be used as well. There might be a cesspit in the garden for the servants, and stool-closets for the family around the house, or

Long-case clocks combined precision engineering with woodwork marquetry of the highest craftsmanship. This example is by Charles Gretton, who was apprenticed in 1662, and in 1700 became a master clockmaker with premises in Fleet Street.

sometimes even on the roof. These had to be emptied regularly by servants. Despite these arrangements, it was not unknown for bursting men and women to relieve themselves in the fireplace: Pepys recorded incidents of surprising female guests in the act, somewhat to their embarrassment but not at all to his disgust. Few houses had bathrooms, and a visit to the public baths, or a wash in a copper tub in a private chamber, were the usual ways to get clean.

All but the poorest had a servant of some kind, for the housework or to look after the household's horses. Many were young: girls might be hired as domestic servants or chambermaids, and boys as stable-hands and general helpers. Such servants would be hired for a year at a time, but other valued servants, such as cooks or personal servants might remain with the same family for decades. With long hours (sometimes on laundry day a servant had to get up as early as 1 a.m. to begin the long process of soaking the dirty linen in a ley of ashes and urine before thoroughly rinsing and drying), low pay and no security, a servant's quality of life depended on winning the respect and trust of the master and mistress. A few wealthier families – notably those of ships' captains or with lands in the Americas – might have a young African slave; sometimes when the family portrait was painted this slave was included, suggesting that he was treated as a kind of exhibit, to be put on show. The rights under common law of a slave brought to England were much disputed.

A grand gilded and lacquered cabinet of the kind favoured by the owners of the largest houses of the period.

Many families kept animals. According to Daniel Defoe, most houses had a cat, maybe five or six. Many also kept dogs, whether for working (some small dogs were used as turnspits, running endlessly round a treadmill to turn the spits used to roast meat by the fire) or as fashion accessories – Charles II made spaniels popular, while pugs were too; some fashionable women liked to carry small dogs in the fur muffs in which they kept their hands warm. Samuel Pepys kept canaries and a blackbird, and knew people with pet monkeys; unlike many others though, he chose not to own a horse but borrowed or hired one when he needed it.

This was an age of gardening, and even the most urban areas had gardens for profit and delight, as well as vegetable patches in the immediate

A view of the docks and community at Deptford in 1690, where John Evelyn lived.

vicinity. On his return from exile Charles II brought with him the French taste for a grand formal garden, but even those who would or could not design on this scale took pleasure in both overall garden design and in tending individual plants. Many, like the diarist John Evelyn, found gardening a source of endless fascination and pleasure.

Opposite bottom: The Privy Garden of Hampton Court was designed in the Baroque style in 1702, and carefully restored in the 1990s to its original intended appearance.

Left: Jordans Quaker Meeting House, in Buckinghamshire, was built in 1685. Its simple panelling and furniture was far removed from the ornate classical architecture of Wren's Anglican churches.

Some, who found the political twists and turns of the era too hard to follow, chose to retire from the world of affairs to their gardens, and a new literature emerged of the delights of the rural retreat. New plants like the pineapple were introduced to Britain from exotic parts of the world. Many of England's towns boasted nurseries on their outskirts, and the proprietors produced catalogues advertising their wares: seeds and seedlings for plants and flowers both ornamental and useful. Gardens were formal in design, with neatly kept hedges. The long cold winters restricted the range of plants that would grow satisfactorily in England, though the very wealthiest had summerhouses, orangeries and glasshouses in which to grow vines or other warm-climate plants.

It was also an age of church-building, especially in London after the Fire, where Christopher Wren himself was responsible for over fifty new churches. The fiercely enforced Anglican orthodoxy which was imposed after the Restoration gave little room for alternatives. Some non-conformist groups tried to continue meeting but were forbidden to do so within five miles of a town. Those who stood against this were subject to ridicule, disruption or persecution, including long and repeated spells in prison.

Overleaf: The great hall of Bolsover Castle, Derbyshire, created by William Cavendish after much of the original castle had been destroyed in the Civil War. Typically of great houses of this period, the hall is no longer the main room of the house, but an entrance leading to the other accommodation.

WORK

A T A TIME when people began to value reason more highly than ever before, some thinkers tried to conduct a rational study of society itself. William Petty was one of the first economists to use statistics to analyse the wealth of the country, working out in 1665 that an average income was £6 13s 4d. In similar vein, in 1688 Gregory King produced a study of the people of England, in which he made estimates of how many people there were at every rank of society, from lords, baronets and squires down to cottagers, vagrants and common soldiers, and the annual household income of each group. Despite the inevitable shortcomings of the information on which such estimates were based, such men produced the first overall surveys of the conditions of life. Previously, by contrast, pictures of life in England contained in reports produced by foreign ambassadors were often based on their personal observation – such as a frequent comment at this time that even the poor in England could afford shoes and ate white bread.

That Petty and King could conduct such surveys at all indicates that this was an age of the civil servant, a time when people would apply their brains to the public good through administrative ends – what King called 'persons in offices'. Samuel Pepys was another who contributed to this trend, doing much in his role as Secretary to the Navy to rationalise and modernise the provision of the navy, and making it possible to supply everything the navy needed to keep ships at sea for months at a time.

Perhaps similar to the twenty-first century, the last decades of the seventeenth century saw the rise of a financial services industry, where many made a living from running small banks, from insurance and lending money, and buying and selling shares – 'stock-jobbing', a profession which became notorious for its unscrupulousness and greed. The 1690s were a boom-time for this market, as the government engaged in ever more expensive wars and in 1694 was

Opposite:
The milkmaid, carrying a churn on her head and with several jugs: a common sight in the streets of many towns. This and other similar illustrations in this chapter come from the publication *Crys of London* (1688), by Pierce Tempest.

forced to establish the Bank of England to handle its debts. Others made huge amounts of money by administering ('farming') the taxes that the government imposed to pay its debts – especially a poll tax, customs and excise duty raised on alcohol.

The rise of the financial industry, combined with the growth of major investments in hugely profitable overseas trade in both the East and the Americas, saw the emergence of a new class that had made its wealth from money itself. King estimated there were maybe ten thousand such families (including those less wealthy merchants engaged in essentially domestic trade). This was the beginning of a long-term shift that eventually saw power drain away from the nobility, who owned the land but worked little. This group comprised around a thousand families, according to King, with an average annual income of over £1,000.

King also counted ten thousand lawyers and clergymen. Every village had its church, and London alone had a hundred, each one supported by the inhabitants of its tiny parish. A clergyman was recorded as having an annual income of a relatively low £40; but

Godfrey Kneller's portrait of three young aristocrats sharing a decanter of wine exemplifies the chasm between rich and poor at this period.

A servant offers fish to the housewife to select as her husband comes in after a long day. Painting by the Dutch artist Q. G. van Brekelenkam, 1664.

these men, together with the squires who acted as justices of the peace, kept the wheels of local society turning and ensured that the law and the established faith were recognised in every corner of the country.

Farmers gather a good corn harvest in the foreground of a view of Cambridge drawn by Johannes Kip in about 1700.

The Tichborne Dole (1671), by Gillis van Tilborgh, shows an ancient annual ceremony in which the lord and lady of the manor of this Hampshire village bestowed gifts of flour on needy villagers.

In contrast he found over 300,000 households of farmers and freeholders (small farmers), 40,000 shopkeepers and 60,000 artisans. Outstripping all of these were 364,000 families of labourers, 400,000 cottagers and paupers – people whom he considered to be detracting from the wealth of the nation (unlike those above, all of whom he believed added to its annual profits).

By that calculation, roughly three-quarters of the population worked the land, much as they had always done, and together with the ancillary agricultural trades – like smithing and milling – this suggests that perhaps eighty per cent lived in villages or hamlets. However, this certainly did not mean that they were farming at a subsistence level, and foreign visitors often commented on the general prosperity of the country, and how well-fed and well-dressed people were. Many regions had their own specialist produce which had a national market: cattle in Cheshire and the Welsh Marches; turkeys in East Anglia; corn in the Fens, which somewhat counteracted the depressing effect of a slow fall in agricultural prices throughout the period which drove down wages and resulted in rural riots in the 1690s when bread prices started to rise.

Farming practices changed relatively little in these years though some landlords resumed the business of enclosing common land for their own benefit, resulting in local examples of protest or despair, such as maiming the livestock of the lord, or breaking down his fences. Many landlords, though, tried to maintain a sense of their traditional paternal authority, as expressed in the famous painting of the Tichborne Dole.

Even so, people – and wealth – were beginning to move to the towns, as the growing demand for minerals, textiles and coal began to provide employment possibilities. While London was still almost twenty times the size of the second-biggest city (Norwich), many places were beginning to grow, especially those, like Liverpool or Bristol, with direct access to the sea. Newcastle, for example, was thriving on the demand for coal, which it shipped south to London, and it attracted many labourers from Scotland. The great naval dockyards, Plymouth, Portsmouth, Woolwich and Chatham, were the focus of all kinds of industries supplying the navy, from timber and woodworking to rope-making and food processing. Smaller towns might specialise in particular products: stockings in Nottingham, leather in Leicester, shoes in Northampton.

While men did most of the labouring, the women and children were also kept hard at work. Beyond the vital and exhausting household chores, many women sewed, embroidered or made lace to make extra cash. Children might be apprenticed from the age

Below left: This street vendor from *Crys of London* is selling the *London Gazette*, a government newspaper launched in 1665. It had excellent sources of information; its foreign correspondents were the ambassadors or generals.

Below: This sweep is followed by an apprentice, who would typically be an orphan from a parish school.

of seven. Though the system was in something of a long-term decline, half of all businesses still had one or more apprentices, and to buy an apprenticeship in a highly skilled or profitable trade might cost a boy's parents several hundred pounds. Unlucky orphans brought up at parish expense might be apprenticed to chimney sweeps for far less – and forced into a dangerous job with no prospect of prosperity at the end. Probably half of all apprentices dropped out or ran away before they had completed the seven-year stint, in many cases no doubt to face parental displeasure, in others to begin a footloose existence.

This woodcut depicts a range of crafts in the late seventeenth century.

Most domestic servants were girls in their teens or early twenties. Servants were often hired by the year at Michaelmas (September) or on Lady Day (March), but any who misbehaved (and any who got pregnant – or were made pregnant by the man of the house) were likely to be summarily ejected without notice. Washing clothes, fetching water, heating and cleaning the home and preparing food were all long and arduous tasks, and involved usually the lady of the house as well as the servants.

Although servants could be badly treated, they were thought of as members of the family and in theory the head of the household was responsible for their physical and moral welfare. Thus the entire household would go to church together, each Sunday. As the number of prosperous families rose towards the end of the century, so complaints were heard about the difficulties of finding and keeping servants, and of their rising demands and careless attention to their duties, while more and more servants were prosecuted for stealing from their masters.

For those who could not find regular employment, there was the option of being a day labourer or of becoming a street trader, selling all manner of goods. The street cries had long been a noted aspect of urban life, and earlier in the century Orlando Gibbons had set some of them to music. In much the same spirit, Pierce Tempest published seventy-four drawings of these traders, in a 1688 volume entitled *Crys of London*.

For others, there was the option of selling their bodies. Prostitution was a feature of city life, with thousands of girls, many recently arrived from the country, walking the streets or working in taverns, and many more in brothels. The moral tone of the court made these good years for prostitution, despite the opposition of traditional moralists: in 1668 the city's madams banded together successfully to protest against the apprentices who during the traditional Shrove Tuesday merry-making had trashed many of London's brothels. Towards the end of the century the monarchy tried to suppress prostitution and bands of vigilantes set about rounding up, naming, shaming and fining or imprisoning the girls.

The orange-seller, from *Crys of London*. Oranges were popular fruits, and in April 1664, Pepys noted seeing an orange tree in St James's Park.

FOOD AND DRINK

IN 1674, AFTER TEN YEARS of conflict, the Dutch finally agreed to hand over their colony of New Amsterdam to the English, who had already named it New York. The event summed up how confidently Restoration England's navy and merchant fleet was venturing across the world, challenging the right of the Dutch and Spaniards to rule the waves, whether in the Caribbean, around the coast of Africa, in India and the East Indies, or on the eastern seaboard of North America.

One upshot, for Englishmen and women back home, was the appearance of exotic and tropical produce on their streets. Nell Gwyn, one of Charles II's more popular and less aristocratic mistresses, caught the royal eye while making her living selling oranges to the crowds thronging to the theatre in Drury Lane.

Other new tastes from overseas included sugar from the Caribbean colonies such as Barbados and Jamaica. This was mixed with tea, which was beginning to arrive in East India Company ships (an expensive drink taken politely in drawing rooms without milk in the Chinese fashion), coffee from the Middle East and chocolate (also drunk with hot water, not milk) from the Americas. Pepper was just one of many exotic spices that were craved. Together with Virginian tobacco, demand for these products grew insatiably and contributed hugely to the growth and importance of the merchant fleet, the Royal Navy to protect its routes, and the colonies in which to produce the goods. They also greatly increased the numbers of Africans who were forced to endure the horrors of slavery, as this practice was believed to be essential to make their mass-production viable. As a result, sugar was commonly available in London for a few pence per pound.

Mostly, of course, such new tastes were for the middle and upper classes, who could afford to visit the new coffee houses or acquire the paraphernalia – silver tea- and chocolate-pots, sugar bowls and spoons – of the new consumer tastes. Pepys, for example, began to collect his own set of silver in 1661 when he bought six spoons. Such

Opposite:
In the Kitchen
(1669), by the
Dutch artist
David Teniers.

A social gathering usually involved liberal amounts of ale or wine, and the health of each person present was drunk.

A busy dockyard scene in 1673, painted by Jacob Knyff. The port is probably imaginary. An English flagship is on the right, and beside the quay is a Dutch-built flyboat.

people also acquired an increasing taste for wine, especially a sweet Madeira (red) or sack (white). It was sold by the gallon or barrel, and decanted at home as required. This required its own repertoire of cut-glass bottles, silver labels and so on. As lead and crystal glass manufacture techniques improved, many styles of delicate and beautiful sets of wine glass were seen.

According to the accounts of French and German visitors to England, people seemed to drink more heavily than in most

continental countries, a habit that was turned into a ritual by long bouts of toasting. First the guests would drink the health of the king and then of everyone in the room in turn. Those unable to afford wine drank beer – whether weak or 'small' beer or stronger ale – which might be brewed at home or in a brewhouse which doubled as an inn. As for spirits, the popular brandy imports dried up after 1689 when the outbreak of a long war with France adversely affected trade. To replace them, many local distilleries sprang up, while gin, a drink from Holland, was also introduced and began to establish itself as a notorious and cheap route to oblivion for the poor.

A tea party in an elegant country house, early in the eighteenth century. While coffee was a drink for men, tea was mainly enjoyed by aristocratic women.

In the houses of the well-to-do, the diet was often heavy and protein-rich. Breakfast might consist of cold game pie, herrings or even oysters, while the main meal of the day, eaten at midday and known as dinner, could involve a great deal of elaborately prepared beef, lamb or venison, fish or shellfish and sweetmeats, which commonly included dried fruit and were heavily spiced. Lard, butter and eggs seemed to be essential ingredients to most dishes. Vegetables and salads were regarded very much as supplementary (despite John Evelyn's urging people to take them more seriously), but a dessert course based on cooked fruits and cream might be enjoyed. Puddings were universally popular, whether sweet or savoury. Should a snack be required to sustain a person between meals, bread and cheese was commonly chosen. The evening meal might well be little more than a stomach lining for the alcohol intake.

On special occasions, people ate in a truly prodigious manner. On 26 March 1662, Pepys typically gave 'a pretty dinner' for four guests, and the menu comprised 'a brace of stewed carps, six roasted chicken and a jowl of salmon hot, for the first course – a tanzy and two neats' [ox] tongues and cheese the second.'

At a meal in the home of a well-to-do family, the man sat at the head of the table while the woman carved the joint. After 1688 the Dutch style of seating the guests became fashionable, with men and

Opposite top: This woodcut shows a man wearing a turban with a formidable array of pipes, and a black servant pouring the drinks. The nation's insatiable taste for tobacco had fuelled the rise in the use of African slaves on the Virginian plantations.

women alternated. Books of table manners sold well as people realised their importance: Hannah Woolley's *The Gentlewoman's Companion* (1673) was a typical example, advising on everything from how to serve the meat (pass the dish to your most important guests first) to how to pick your teeth at table (don't). This regularly reprinted volume also included a large number of recipes both everyday and elaborate, homely medicines, advice on housekeeping, form letters for every occasion, advice on conversation, deportment and fashions.

A special dinner party might cost a man like Pepys up to £5, but economist Gregory King estimated that a modest person of the middling sort might spend only between £5 and £20 a year on food and drink per person, in total. For such people, simpler fare, based on grains, was the order of the day. Pottage, pease pudding or stew, which might be bulked out with brown bread, supplemented the cheaper cuts of meat. Even so, meat would be regularly served even at an almshouse, where the very poorest lived on the charity of others.

Fresh ingredients were bought from street traders or market stalls, and in the cities a bell would be rung at sunrise to summon people to the market before the wholesalers and other shopkeepers were allowed in. Even a woman of the status of Elizabeth Pepys would go there at 5 a.m., with her servants in tow. After the Fire of London, the food markets were centralised on Leadenhall and Smithfield for meat – Leadenhall had no fewer than one hundred stalls selling nothing but beef, as well as lamb and poultry specialists. Animals destined for market were brought to the city on foot (sometimes from hundreds of miles away) and slaughtered on the spot. Covent Garden was similarly

This still life (*c.* 1700) by Adriaen de Gryeff depicts the produce of an idealised kitchen garden being enjoyed by various wild animals. At a time when resources were scarce, all kinds of birds and wild animals were classed as vermin, and villagers were paid for every rabbit, crow, hedgehog and sparrow they killed.

the focus for vegetables and Billingsgate for fish. Other day-to-day items were sold by itinerants: hawkers sold fruit or shellfish, while milkmaids walked the streets with churns slung across their shoulders, even though milk was rarely drunk fresh, and people preferred to give whey or buttermilk – the by-products of cheese- and butter-making – to the young and sick. Butter was liberally applied to meat and vegetables, rather than to bread. Easy access to cheap sugar increasingly encouraged people to preserve fruit as candies or as jam.

Everyone, rich or poor, ate around a pound of bread a day (which was also the soldier's ration and might cost one penny). For the wealthiest, this was made from white flour or wheaten (and stamped with a W), whereas other folk had brown bread made from grist (stamped with an H, for housewife). Both were made with leaven and baked in the round. The very poorest might find their grist mixed with other grains or bulked out with dried vegetables (unless an unscrupulous baker risked mixing in something worse, like brick-dust). In some towns civic authorities tried to control the price and quality of bread, but it was an unending battle and in rural areas it was impossible.

Not everyone had access to their own cooking facilities. Such people might eat cheaply in victualling houses or inns. And even those who had kitchens might not be able to afford the regular expense of keeping a bread-oven hot, and relied instead on a baker, to whom they might also take the pies they had prepared at home. It was common to have a huge roast of beef on a Sunday, which would be cooked on a spit perhaps turned by a small dog; and they would eat the leftovers cold or otherwise prepared throughout the rest of the week. Fridays were designated as days for eating fish, and proclamations were issued to this effect, as well as to ban the eating of meat during Lent. The fact that these proclamations were necessary suggests that the old custom was not as strictly enforced as the fishing industry might have wished – indeed Pepys's party mentioned above was held during Lent.

Below: Restoration-period equipment for thirst-quenching, decorated with loyal imagery and inspirational mottoes.

Shopping and Style

IT WAS A MERCENARY AGE. People were motivated by money – getting it, keeping it, investing it, flaunting it and spending it – in a way that was quite new. Gold coins for guineas, half-guineas, crowns and half-crowns, and silver for denominations down to sixpence, were made in the Royal Mint in the Tower of London. They were of high quality and were milled (serrated) to get round the ancient problem of clipping off the edges. And though bank notes had yet to be introduced, the rise of the financial industry led to an increase in the use of promissory notes that could be bought and sold.

For everyday purposes, though, coins of smaller denominations were required, and these had been in perpetual short supply since early in the seventeenth century. As a result, many traders opted to create their own 'tokens' of lead, tin or copper which would eventually be collected and redeemed for coins of the realm. After the Fire of 1666, however, this unofficial system was thrown into disarray and eventually the Royal Mint started issuing copper farthings and halfpennies.

Money could buy most things, at least in the cities where prostitution was rife, and where the moral restraint imposed by a fear of eternal damnation was in decline. This was the first great age of shopping, and fashionable shops could be found along the Strand, around the Royal Exchange in the City and even in Westminster Hall. Many older shops had shutters, which opened downwards to form a counter that projected onto the street. The new style of shops introduced fixed windows, doors and an internal counter. Mirrors and light fittings

Opposite:
Lady at her Toilette (1660) by the Dutch artist Gerard ter Borch.

Left:
Money, then as now, made the world go round. The improvements in the quality and quantity of the coins from the Royal Mint stabilised economic confidence for many.

43

A notice advertising a forthcoming book auction, with many of the titles written on the books themselves.

created a bright interior. All this allowed for the development of the window display, which might be accompanied by a billboard or hoarding. According to Daniel Defoe, writing just after the turn of the century, a high-class shopkeeper might spend the unheard-of sum of £500 in fitting out his shop before opening for business. Many advertised their wares by means of handbills; others preferred to have runners – perhaps young girls – outside to tempt in the customers.

Beyond the basic necessities of life, shops for all kinds of consumer goods were to be found – tobacco and snuff, hats and canes, clocks and watches, as well as furniture and decorative objects for the home, books, spectacles and patent medicines. The most important, though, were cloth and clothes.

Tailors able to offer the latest styles – usually inspired by what was being worn in Paris – were most sought-after, and the royal court set the tone, first through Charles and his many women, and in the 1690s through Queen Mary II. She was renowned as a follower of fashion who might buy several pairs of shoes each week, and had luxuriously

A draper's shop in the 1690s, painted by E. J. van Heemskerk. The shopkeeper is sitting on the left while a porter holds a bale of cloth; there are two clients at the back, one with a tally stick. Beyond the door is a wholesale vintner, where three men examine the contents of a wine-glass.

embroidered underwear. Husbands and would-be husbands continually complained about the cost of meeting the fashionable tastes of their womenfolk. A lady would normally wear a long cotton or linen shift next to the skin. Next would be stays, a form of corset stiffened with whalebone or wood; and finally a gown, with woollen or silk stockings to keep the legs warm.

Portraits of the most fashionable ladies of the period universally show low-cut gowns and yards of silk and ribbons. This was the style called 'undress' and was intended for wearing at home, deriving as it did from the simple nightgown. A more practical loose gown with sleeves, known as a mantua, became popular in the final years of the century. This might be cut open at the front to reveal an embroidered corset, gathered at the waist and with a full skirt, possibly hitched up to reveal a petticoat.

Accessories included folding fans for indoors, large fur muffs, essential for the unusually cold climate of these years, gold and silver thread, and point (lace), which was produced in industrial volumes (lace-making, like stocking-knitting, was a job often done by nimble-fingered children). Jewellery included necklaces – pearls remained much sought-after – rings and diamond earrings. Gold watches were just coming into fashion, but these were still items for show and not yet reliable for telling the time. Out of doors, a woman wore a cloak, and sturdier clothes were needed for travelling or riding. Hats with hatbands were always worn (or simpler coifs for the poor).

A wool-and-silk corset of the 1670s, decorated with gold braid and spangles, and lined with linen.

For the majority of women, for whom leisure was not the way of life, a simple loose jacket or bodice and full woollen skirt, or a front-buttoning one-piece dress might be worn as day-to-day wear. Despite this, there was a general attempt to keep up with the fashions so far as possible, and the old sumptuary laws which had set out what clothes could be worn by each social class had fallen into disuse. Instead, many women endlessly sewed, altering their clothes or making new outfits from the cast-offs of the wealthier set.

Men's clothes were a mixture of the splendid and the practical. In 1663 John Evelyn reported seeing a man in Westminster Hall 'with as much ribbon about him as would have plundered six shops and set up twenty country pedlars. All his body was dress'd like a maypole or a Tom-a-Bedlam cap.' Not all were so foppish. On top of the shirt and

knee-length drawers were worn knee-length breeches, sometimes trimmed with ribbon, and woollen, linen or silk stockings held up by garters. One advantage of the breeches was that they contained internal pockets. Above, a sleeveless waistcoat and cravat might be worn, and on top, a jacket or coat – newly fashionable items that replaced the older habit of wearing a cloak. A second shirt might be worn to keep warm. Lace sleeves, a coloured sash and ruffs added to the display, as did a wide-brimmed, perhaps feathered hat, which was ideally made of beaver, but might be of velvet or felt. Hats were worn out of doors, except in the presence

Above:
A well-dressed couple of the 1660s. He is wearing a long wig, coat, breeches and heeled shoes, and carrying his sword on an ostentatious sash.

of a social superior – hence the outrage when the Quakers, who believed in the equality of all before God, expressed that belief by refusing to go bare-headed when faced with an aristocrat or a judge.

For comfort and indoors, a prosperous man might wear a long gown, perhaps made of imported Indian or Turkish cotton or silk, or a warmer material for the winter. These could be richly decorated. To keep the head warm indoors, he might wear a turban. Shoes were heeled, and might have silver buckles; there was no distinction between left and right foot, and metal or wooden pattens might be used to lift the shoe clean above the mud of the roads and lanes. Men carried canes, walking sticks or swords, and perfumed gloves or muffs. Mouchoirs, or kerchiefs, added a further touch of style.

Women who could afford the time to look after their appearance commonly used makeup. 'To cleanse the skin of the face, and make it look beautiful and fair,' said Hannah Woolley:

Take Rosemary and boil it in White-wine, with the juice of Erigan put thereunto, and wash your face therewith Mornings and Evenings. If your Face be troubled with heat, take Elder-flowers, Plantane, white Daisie roots, and Herb-Robert and put these into running-water, and wash your Face therewith at night, and in the Morning.

The much more unpleasant and dangerous ceruse, a lead-based white paste, was used for pock-marks and other major blemishes. Cochineal offered a touch of rouge for the cheeks, and crayons coloured the lips and eyelids. Finally a few patches – black beauty-spots – were stuck on with gum.

Women and men probably washed hands and face daily, but also sometimes bathed, perhaps in a public bathhouse, though these were places of uncertain reputation. Hannah Woolley and other writers paid particular attention to techniques of dealing with under-arm body odour and advocated rubbing the teeth with rosemary blossom, brine or 'Mr. Turners Dentifrices, which are every-where much cryed up' to deal with bad breath. Underwear was washed regularly, but outerwear was usually brushed clean. Ordinary people kept a best set of clothes for Sundays, and used working clothes the rest of the week.

Men were mainly clean-shaven – a task they might do themselves when they felt short of cash, or leave to the barber, but probably not every day. In the 1660s, a fashion for shaven heads, to be covered by periwigs, was introduced – apparently by the king, who had turned prematurely grey. Over the following decades these became more and more expensive and ungainly. Wigs were made of human hair, and had to be regularly set: on occasion a man might remove his wig in public to brush it. Wigs – even more so than living hair – were perennially lice-infested. A fine wig, though, instantly identified someone as a man of standing, and a potential target for pickpockets – who might even snatch the wig itself from his head.

Women generally sported their own hair, but by the 1690s the fashion was for a huge bouffant 'commode', arranged around a wire frame, and set off with curls around the ears and forehead. For most, though, this was absurdly complex, and far too difficult to keep up with the array of combs which were all that was available, so a more natural style was worn, with loose curls whenever possible. The ideal beauty was raven-black hair framing a pale face.

Both men and women wore long nightshirts and embroidered caps to bed.

Opposite bottom: Queen Mary II (r. 1689–94) came to the throne after the expulsion of her father James II. She was known as a dedicated follower of fashion, as well as setting an example of piety and devotion in her court.

A gentleman in blue velvet, portrait by Godfrey Kneller painted around 1700.

Trade to Harborough

You that delight to take up foreign Linnen,
At Harb'rough made, a little Town in Bremen,
Encourage Trade abroad for time to come
And like Kind Fools, neglect your own at home.

TRANSPORT

E NGLAND'S NETWORK OF ROADS AND RIVER-BRIDGES was already centuries old by the late seventeenth century, and these years saw little alteration or addition to the country's infrastructure. Almost all roads between towns, whether main or minor, were narrow, twisting, unpaved and rutted, and travel along them was laborious and uncomfortable. Signposts were few and far between. Indeed, over the previous hundred years the roads had got worse, as traffic increased and as the number of heavy wagons grew. A person could manage around twenty miles a day on foot, or double that on horseback, but heavy wagons, pulled by a team of up to eight horses might do little more than ten miles in the same time. Bad weather could close roads entirely.

Traditionally, each parish or town was responsible for the upkeep of its own roads and bridges, but the expense was burdensome and the appalling condition of the roads was coming to be seen to be a national issue. In this period an attempt was made to co-ordinate effort. In 1663, Parliament tried to get the users of the Great North Road to contribute to its maintenance by erecting a number of tollbooths along the route, and similar schemes were tried elsewhere: these later turned into the turnpike trusts which were to revolutionise road transport in the next century.

Wealthy people were choosing to keep printed and beautiful maps of the country, both for practical and decorative reasons, and almanacs setting out the details of the route were popular: the mapmaker John Ogilby, for example, published descriptions of many journeys across England with strip maps for the traveller's convenience.

The condition of the roads was indicative of the growing wealth and complexity of English society. Across the country more and more farmers were investing in carts, a clear indicator of the importance of commerce, rather than mere subsistence, while in most towns there were hauliers making their living by carrying raw materials and manufactured goods to market, many of them keeping a score of horses and several wagons.

Opposite:
This playing card depicts a trading vessel importing linen from Bremen in northern Germany.

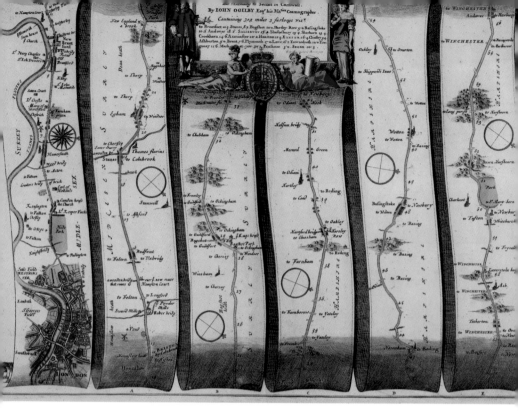

John Ogilby produced this strip map of the road from London to Andover, and ultimately to Land's End, in 1675.

People of all classes needed to travel: to get raw materials or to take goods to market, to pursue legal or social interests, education or military activity. Some travelled to further the government's business. The 1660s also saw the development of the country's postal service, which had begun earlier in the century. Initially restricted to government business, it was now made available to the public, though the cost meant that it was not yet a service for the masses. Whereas the earliest services had been between London, Plymouth, York, Edinburgh and Dublin, the national network was now growing with many smaller distribution centres. In 1680 a local penny-post was introduced in London, an innovation later seen in other towns.

Such a service required infrastructure, in the form of inns where a postmaster could ensure that teams of horses were ready for the couriers who were delivering the mail. These inns became the nodes for the entire transport system, places that horses could be hired privately, or stopping points for the developing stagecoach system. Scheduled services were now available, costing around 2d per mile, but they were slow and extremely uncomfortable, with up to eight passengers squeezed inside unsprung carriages, and others in a large open basket at the back or on the roof. Such coaches might cover fifty miles in a day.

Other travellers preferred private transport. Celia Fiennes spent twenty years between 1684 and 1703 riding side-saddle around the country alone or with just a servant or two, as she said, 'to regain my health by variety and change of aire and exercise'. Her account of her journey presents an incomparable portrait of the country in the last decades of the century, and she is thought to have been the first woman to visit every county in England. She, at least, was not deterred by the highwaymen who were an ever-present danger for the stagecoaches.

Private coaches were also becoming more comfortable. Pepys, for example, who was happy to hire a horse whenever he wanted to ride either within London or for a day out in the country, proudly bought himself a coach in 1668 (for £53 – more than Gregory King's estimate of a typical clergyman's annual stipend, so perhaps equivalent to the price of a luxury car today). The introduction of glass windows, and sprung suspension in the following decades began to make coach travel a little more pleasant (though it was not unknown for even the king's coach to overturn), while the development of the light two-wheeled gig offered a much speedier option.

Within the city, hackney carriages were available for casual hire, and the first licences were given in London in 1662. They were used much as we use taxis today, and the rates, established by Act of

The country's network of inns acted as focal points for the transportation system. The George Hotel in Dorchester-on-Thames dates from the fifteenth century, making it one of the oldest coaching inns in the country. Among its contemporary guests was Sarah Churchill, first Duchess of Marlborough.

Left: A modest coach.

Below: A 1690 procession in The Hague of William III, stadtholder of the Netherlands as well as king of England and Scotland. The low-slung, roofed coaches were the most comfortable of the day.

Parliament, were 1/6d for the first hour, and 1/— thereafter, and up to six customers might share the fare. Hackney carriage drivers soon established a reputation for rudeness that they have never quite shaken off.

But many people simply walked. Pepys, for example, thought nothing of walking for ten miles or more a day; and his description of the Fire of London includes a vivid account of wealthy men carrying their beds or other precious possessions on their backs as they fled the city.

For those who did not even want to walk, or could not do so, there was the option to be carried by two porters in a glass-windowed sedan

within the city, something Celia Fiennes described as being particularly popular with the infirm and the well-dressed. Sedans were both more comfortable and more manoeuvrable in the crowded narrow streets than a carriage, and were common in fashionable spas such as Bath. There were regular complaints that sedan-bearers would unceremoniously knock other pedestrians out of the way.

Somewhat more comfortable and faster than any kind of road transport – though equally exposed to the elements – was to take to the water. In a great city such as London, watermen would offer short rides across or along the river. Wherries offered regular passenger services within London and from the surrounding counties, while smaller skiffs could be hired for private use. Some contemporary commentators estimated there were over ten thousand such boats plying their trade on the Thames. The royal family, aristocracy and the city travelled in style up the river in fine barges, perhaps with musical accompaniment. Less exalted barges carried heavy goods up and down the rivers to towns throughout the land, suggesting a huge supply of steady muscle power to keep the country going. In some places this had to be imported: in Newcastle, for example, a notorious community of Scots grew up to row the coal down the Tyne, and place it on the sea-going ships that carried it down to the capital.

As England became ever more reliant on the sea, ports serviced saltwater craft of every size, whether local fishing vessels, coastal traffic, transatlantic traders or the growing naval vessels which protected the shipping lanes. Destructive but unresolved wars were fought with the other great maritime people of the age – the Dutch – for control of the Channel and the right to carry English and colonial trade in English ships. Provisioning – and financing – the navy became an industry in its own right, one with Pepys, as Secretary to

The arrival in Portsmouth of Catherine of Braganza to marry Charles II in May 1662 was the occasion for a great procession of highly decked-out barges.

Abbildung wie die Königin von Groß Britanien, zu Portsmouth angelangt ift. den 2 5 May Ann

the Navy, at its heart. English shipbuilding skills were sufficiently renowned for Peter 'the Great', Tsar of Russia, to visit in order to study them and take the knowledge back to his native land. Shipbuilding promoted all kinds of ancillary industries and crafts, including timber, rope-making, canvas manufacture, barrel-making, iron-founding and much else besides. The importance of the sea and the navy was recognised by the creation of the royal hospital for sailors at Greenwich in 1694. The importance – and the romance – of the sea was also recognised by the popularity of marine paintings, a style introduced from Holland in which the viewpoint is often right at the level of the water as the sails of merchant or naval vessels billow, confidently riding out turbulent winds.

England's growing cultural and commercial connections with the continent, and involvement in European wars in the Low Countries especially after 1688, meant that traffic in the Channel was busier and easier than ever. A trip to France in clement weather might take just half a day.

Transatlantic traffic was growing, too, with several new colonies created in North America requiring thousands of inhabitants and the

The navy was vital to English life, and the Royal Naval Hospital at Greenwich was founded in 1694 for sailors and their families.

shipping out of all the provisions necessary to establish a new society, and to bring back the raw materials they produced. These years also saw the growth of the infamous 'triangular trade' of slaves to the Caribbean and North America, as well as ever more adventurous trading and military expeditions to India and beyond. Western ports, such as Bristol and Liverpool, thrived as never before. The journey to the New World was expected to take a month, and was a daunting prospect. In addition to the usual discomforts and dangers of the sea there was the new threat of piracy: this was the great age of the privateer and freebooter preying on unprotected shipping in the Caribbean and off the American eastern seaboard.

Of those who made a living at sea, some like Henry Morgan became pirates and established a good living, and a fearsome reputation, based in Jamaica. He died in his bed, in London, in 1688.

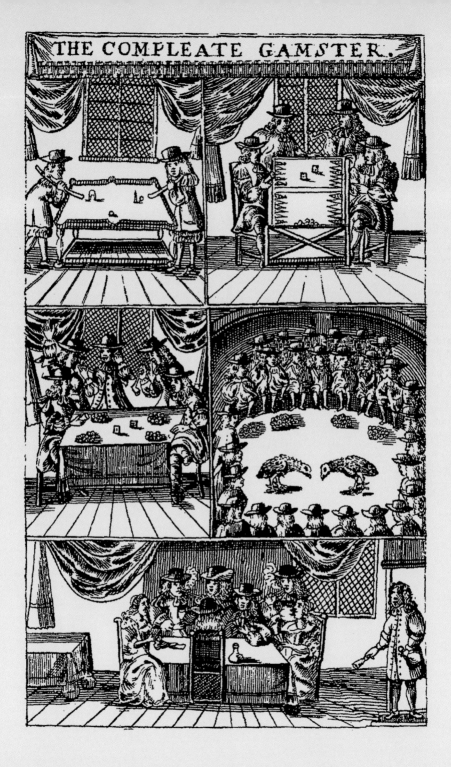

ENTERTAINMENT

MERRY-MAKING was back after the puritan rigours of the republican years. Notoriously, celebrating Christmas had been banned, as had alehouses and the theatre. With the king leading the way in showing people how to enjoy themselves, all were now back with a vengeance, and the enthusiastic celebrations of his return in May 1660 showed how willing the people were to follow his lead. While much entertainment naturally could be had in private comfort at home or with friends, much more was available in the public sphere and had to be paid for.

New theatres, or playhouses, were built, and these resembled modern theatres in being roofed and with a proscenium arch carrying a curtain that was drawn back for the performance. The finest, such as the Theatre Royal, Drury Lane, were designed by Christopher Wren. On stage, simple flat painted scenery was used. Seats were available in the stalls, in the gallery or in boxes, and it was necessary to arrive several hours before a popular show to secure a seat. The audience could be rowdy throughout the performance, which normally began in mid-afternoon, with the stage lit by daylight boosted by candles. Unlike in Shakespeare's day, the audience tended to be mainly better-off people or members of the court.

As well as Shakespeare, licentious or romantic comedies were popular, with William Congreve the best-known playwright of the day; his 1695 play *Love For Love* was a smash hit. In the 1660s, women were allowed to act for the first time, frequently in parts that involved dressing as a man. Elizabeth Barry and Susanna Verbruggen won huge reputations, as did Thomas Betterton in conventional male roles. Many moralists denounced the immorality of the stage, with clergyman Jeremy Collier publishing an influential pamphlet called *A Short View of the Immorality and Profaneness of the English Stage* in 1698.

A little less rumbustious were the coffee houses. The first had opened in Oxford in 1650, and by 1700 there were two thousand in

Opposite: Aristocratic pastimes of the 1670s included billiards, backgammon, dice, cockfighting and cards. Fortunes changed hands in all of them.

Above:
The stage of the Dorset Garden Theatre, with proscenium arch and painted scenery, in 1673. The auditorium had stalls, a gallery and two tiers of boxes and could seat 850 people. The theatre opened in 1671 and was knocked down in 1709.

Above right:
The coffee house was the place of choice for men to relax, talk, eat and do business.

London alone, and many more in towns large and small across the nation. These were exclusively places for men to meet, smoke, drink, do business, eat and talk around a large common table. The walls were often plastered with advertisements for local businesses. Each coffee house had its own regular clientele, and many operated a set of rules, with forfeits for gambling, swearing, arguing or discussing religion or politics, for example. Yet, with many operating as informal offices (Lloyd's insurance house began in a coffee house in 1691, for example), and others as places where men with leisure and cash to spare came to keep up with gossip and debate the great affairs of the day as they appeared in the tri-weekly newspapers (newly popular after the Licensing Act lapsed in 1695), they became known as places of free speech where the enforcement of such rules was often unrealistic. In 1675 the king, anxious about the rising criticism of his regime, issued a proclamation to suppress coffee houses altogether, but never dared put it into effect.

May Day was once again an opportunity for morris dancing and frolicking around the maypole; on St John's Eve, which coincided with Midsummer, bonfires, fairs and parades were enjoyed; and Guy Fawkes Day, 5 November, became a huge popular expression of anti-Catholicism, combining church services, bell-ringing, fireworks and drinking. The twelve days of Christmas were celebrated too and served as the nearest thing most people had to an annual holiday, an opportunity to eat and drink and generally let off steam. The Yule Log was lit and would remain alight for the rest of the holiday, much wassailing (communal singing and passing around a wassail bowl of spiced ale) took place and mince pies, goose or turkey and plum porridge were enjoyed at the feast on 25 December. Presents were exchanged on New Year's Day; and more revelries occurred on Twelfth Night, when an elaborate spiced cake was served and a lord of misrule appointed to oversee the fun. The first Monday after Twelfth Night was Plough Monday, and in rural districts plough teams would decorate the plough with ribbons and knock up all the houses in the village before starting the year's work.

These were not the only occasions for letting hair down. The two-week-long Bartholomew Fair, held in London at the end of August, featured sideshows, rides, street entertainers and foodstalls, and was much disapproved of by the city authorities; Shrove Tuesday was another day of regular rowdyism, especially on the part of the apprentices who would engage in rough games around the town. These might include football, which was played up and down the streets, particularly on the coldest days of winter when traffic was

The Observator was one of a breed of new political broadsheets. Published by Roger L'Estrange in the early 1680s, it mainly comprised rhetoric attacking the King's enemies, the Whigs.

lighter than usual. A blown-up pig's bladder was used for the ball. It was not uncommon for windows – especially the new sash style – to get broken. In the country, games might be played between villages, and with no set pitch the game could range far and wide.

Other noisy entertainments included bull- or bear-baiting and cockfighting, which attracted large crowds and (like all sports) serious gambling. But the greatest street theatre of all was on execution days in London when criminals were taken by cart from the city's prisons to Tyburn Hill, an event in which the more nonchalant among the condemned conspired to provide fine entertainment, with repartee, drunkenness and high emotion amongst both the protagonists and the crowd. On one occasion Pepys was prepared to part with a shilling in order to buy himself a decent view of the proceedings.

Slightly less lethal sports included wrestling, most popular among the lower orders, while boxing – with bare knuckles and few rules – was also beginning to appear. Athletic competitions of strength, agility, speed and endurance were popular in both town and country, whether formally organised or not. Ball games, too, were growing in popularity, though they were often regional in their appeal. As well as football there was cricket in rural southern England, sponsored by the local nobleman who might offer a prize of up to fifty guineas to the winning team; stowball or stoolball (a game with some similarities

Opposite: Public executions, at Tyburn Hill or elsewhere, were a reliable source of entertainment for those who could attend, and of news reports for those who could not be there in person. In this case (1663) the central part was played by a wealthy merchant whose extravagant lifestyle had been paid for by a theft of diamonds, sapphires and rubies.

Individual racehorses acquired celebrity, none more so than the Byerly Turk. This Arab stallion was reputedly captured at the battle of Buda in 1686, and ridden by an army officer at the battle of the Boyne in 1690. His progeny went on to become the first thoroughbreds.

to baseball) was played in Wiltshire and the West Country; golf in Scotland; and Pall Mall, an energetic version of croquet, was played in St James's Park in London and gave its name to the Mall. Bowls, skittles and ninepins and their variations were similarly popular and usually enjoyed at an alehouse. Indoors, dice and playing cards provided entertainment – and the chance to win a fortune – to all classes, and packs of cards were printed with graphic political messages that could be understood by literate and illiterate alike. Gambling, like noisier entertainments, was forbidden on Sundays, though in all likelihood few were deterred by that.

Another sport on which fortunes were won and lost was horseracing, and the most prestigious track was at Newmarket. As part of her dowry, Charles II's queen Catherine of Braganza brought to England some mares from Tangier whose offspring were bred with an Arab stallion called The Byerly Turk, which had been brought to England in 1689. The mixing of their genes would result in the first thoroughbreds. The King himself took great pleasure in racing:

Music and dancing were accomplishments expected of any upwardly mobile couple; Samuel and Elizabeth Pepys both took lessons. This painting is by Pieter de Hooch.

he not only gave the prize and wrote the rules for the Newmarket Town Plate but, in 1675, managed to win it himself on a horse called Blew Capp.

More genteel were drawing, music and dancing. These accomplishments were energetically pursued by those who wanted to appear cultured. Many people were familiar with country dances – jigs and reels – but Charles II introduced fashionable styles from France and foreign dancing-masters were highly sought-after, as were music teachers. Printed instructions were available for those without a live teacher. Professional musicians were an interesting novelty of the age, with public concerts given at several venues in London, performing the music of Henry Purcell and many continental composers. Outdoor concerts were given in Kensington and in the public pleasure gardens of Vauxhall Gardens and the royal parks such as Hyde Park. Such places combined formal walkways and planting in the style of Versailles or Het Loo with more informal wooded parkland, and allowed people to take the air and be seen. Those in search of curiosity could visit the royal menagerie in the Tower of London to ogle the pelicans, hawks and lions (the elephant died in 1660 and was not replaced), but in 1686 the daughter of one of the keepers was mauled to death. Other similar public spectacles were available in other towns – while in Oxford in 1683 the first public museum opened, the Ashmolean. Those who sought out such cerebral pleasures might also attend anatomical dissections (taking a steady supply of models from the ranks of executed criminals) or scientific lectures.

But in these, the years of the 'little Ice Age', when it was common for the rivers to freeze solid, the most famous entertainment was the frost fair. In the winter of 1683–84, the River Thames was frozen for weeks and the ice was almost a foot thick. At such times, boats were fitted with skates and stalls were set up on the ice in mid-river, with food, shops and games. John Evelyn described the scene:

> Coaches plied from Westminster to the Temple, and from several other stairs too and fro, as in the streets; sleds, sliding with skeetes, a bull-baiting, horse and coach races, puppet plays and interludes, cooks, tipling and other lewd places, so that it seemed to be a bacchanalian triumph, or carnival on the water.

Another eyewitness claimed an ox was roasted on the ice. How much melting resulted is not recorded.

Overleaf:
Frost fairs were held whenever the ice was deemed strong enough. The narrow spans of London Bridge tended to make floating ice back up and form a solid surface capable of holding not just men and women, but boats (to which sled runners might be attached, to keep them upright), carriages and cattle.

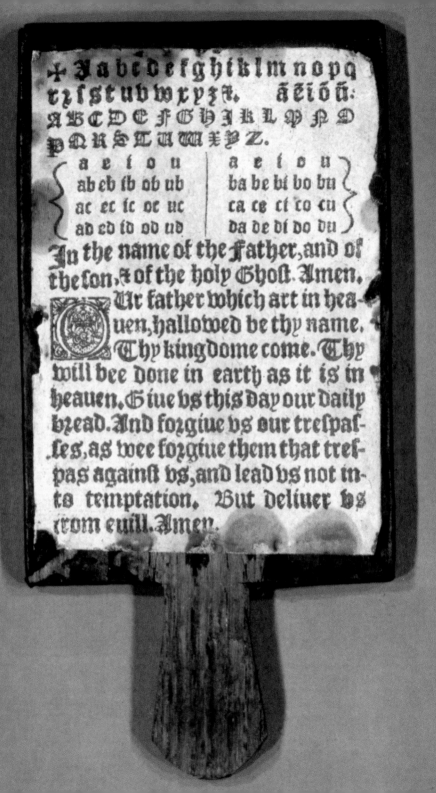

✠ Ꝛ a b c d e f g h i k l m n o p q
r ꞅ ſ s t u b w x y z ꝫ.   ā ē ī ō ū:
A B C D E F G H I K L M N O
P Q R S T U W X Y Z.

a e i o u	a e i o u
ab eb ib ob ub	ba be bi bo bu
ac ec ic oc uc	ca ce ci co cu
ad ed id od ud	da de di do du

In the name of the Father, and of
the Son, ✠ of the holy Ghoſt. Amen.

Ur father which art in heauen, hallowed be thy name.
Thy kingdome come. Thy
will bee done in earth as it is in
heauen. Giue vs this day our daily
bread. And forgiue vs our trespaſ-
ſes, as wee forgiue them that tref-
pas againſt vs, and lead vs not into temptation. But deliuer vs
from euill. Amen.

EDUCATION AND SOCIAL SERVICE

HISTORIANS have long debated the extent to which people were able to read and write. It depends what you mean: a recent survey has concluded that almost half the men and a quarter of the women in the country could write their own names by 1700, though a far higher proportion could do so in the cities, and fewer in country areas. Quite possibly more people could read, at least to some extent.

Many boys and girls received their first education at 'petty school' (junior school) from the age of five, where they learned their letters and numbers, using hornbooks, or sheets of paper pasted onto flat wooden paddles. Many such schools were run by the parish, with no dedicated building, and the teacher (who might be the vicar himself) required no special training.

After petty school, most girls were expected to help around the home or to begin earning their keep; educational opportunities were few and far between, even for the better off, though some girls' schools, teaching both academic subjects and practical skills, existed in the larger towns (Hannah Woolley ran one in Hackney, east London). Other education would have been confined to catechism – basic religious instruction: as one woman put it in 1661, her daughter's education should comprise: 'learning the Bible, good huswifery, writing and good work: other learning a woman needs not.'

A small proportion of boys, though – those who were not sent off to become apprentices or servants, or immediately set to work as labourers – went on to grammar schools. Located in most towns, these were for boys aged from eight to fifteen, and the children learned the rudiments of Latin and perhaps Greek; some also taught arithmetic and basic science. Christ's Hospital, for example, was given a royal charter in 1673 to teach mathematics and navigation in order to produce future naval officers and merchant seamen. Most grammar schools were free, with scholarships endowed to allow the sons of poorer people to acquire an education.

Opposite: Hornbooks, sheets of paper stuck to horn paddles, were essential materials for teaching reading.

Bluecoat schools were established as charity schools, and derived their name from the uniform, which was typical for apprentices of the time. Christ's Hospital was founded in the sixteenth century; it is shown here in about 1700, around which date several more were founded.

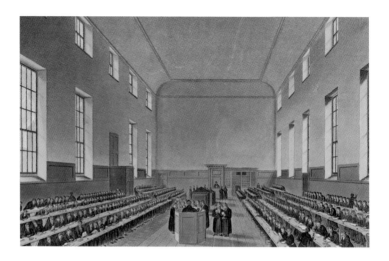

The children of the wealthy might be sent away to boarding school, or alternatively were educated at home, with tutors or governesses employed by the parents. Even here, though, the sexes had a very different education, with the girls concentrating on domestic skills and accomplishments such as music and sewing, rather than academic knowledge. They might for example be taught French, the language of culture and style, rather than Latin, the language of knowledge.

After school, the son of a wealthy family might be sent to Oxford or Cambridge, England's only universities (in Scotland, St Andrews had been founded in 1412). He might stay at university for four years, acquiring an essentially classical education, while enjoying himself in the perennial manner of students everywhere. After this a young gentleman might spend a year or so on the Continent, visiting Paris, Amsterdam or the German or Italian cities. For those who had not such a privileged upbringing, the Inns of Court provided a lawyer's training.

All this was available only to those who accepted the established Anglican church, but from the 1660s the dissenting sects set up their own schools and academies: several Quaker schools were established for example (including two for girls), even while the Society of Friends itself was subject to persecution.

Discipline was often strict, and Hannah Woolley mentions a case in which a governess, 'being somewhat aged, and suspecting her strength was not able to grapple with active youth call'd up her mail to her assistance, with whose help she so cruelly chastised a young Gentlewoman for some fault she had committed, that with grief and shame, she died in a little time after.' But she makes clear that this was

exceptional, and there was a long debate as to the right balance between kindness and severity in the upbringing of children: philosopher John Locke, for example, argued that 'those children who have been most chastised seldom make the best men.'

Those who could read with facility often read a great deal, with religious literature most important. Many families kept a copy of the Bible while the 1662 edition of the *Book of Common Prayer* was placed by law in every church and, like the Bible, resounds with phrases that have been familiar to Britons over the last three centuries. Beyond these, probably the most popular book was John Bunyan's allegory of the Christian life, *The Pilgrim's Progress*, which was written around 1670, and of which twenty editions had been published by 1695. But secular literature was growing in popularity: almanacs which combined a compendium of more or less reliable factual and practical information with tidal tables and the like, sold almost half a million copies a year. Many people were

John Bunyan, as depicted on the title spread of his spiritual masterpiece *The Pilgrim's Progress* (1678), one of the most popular books of this and later centuries.

Wenceslaus Hollar's engraving of London before and after the Fire graphically shows the extent of the devastation.

EEPLE IN SOUTHWARKE IN ITS FLOURISHING CONDITION BEFORE THE FIRE. *designed by W. Hollar of Prag*

ON

The Tower

THAMES

The Bridge

PEARETH NOW AFTER THE SAD CALAMITIE AND DESTRVCTION BY FIRE, in the Yeare M. DC. LXVI

also interested in self-improvement. There was a great deal of curiosity about life on other continents – not surprising perhaps at a time when colonists were actively being sought – and in basic historical knowledge. Books on gardening proliferated, as did household manuals such as Hannah Woolley's.

After a man's education was complete, at whatever level, he was generally free to get on with his life: there was no compulsory social or military service, unless he was unlucky enough to be impressed for the navy, a practice that had been used during the civil wars though discontinued for the army at the Restoration. Other social duties included occasional voting in parliamentary elections – but only for the small number who met the property qualifications. Even then, voting was done in public and an elector could expect to receive a bribe for his pains.

Vestries – the committees responsible for running the affairs of a parish – might be responsible for looking after roads, for rudimentary law enforcement and similar civic functions. Even more important was poor relief, which since 1601 had fallen to the churchwardens and vestry to administer. Some poor relief consisted of doles or one-off payments to support those in need, perhaps to recover their clothes from the pawnbroker. Occasionally these might be paid regularly over a period of years. Those in receipt of such payments had to wear a badge identifying them as recipients, and anti-social behaviour, such as drunkenness or what was called immodesty, could see the payments cut. Other poor people were cared for privately, in almshouses or through other charitable institutions, perhaps endowed by a nobleman or run by a trade guild or livery company for the families of its members who had fallen on hard times.

In addition, a parish or group of parishes might run an orphanage or even a workhouse for the indigent, infirm and aged poor, paid for from rates collected from local residents, and also from the sale of the goods produced by the residents of the workhouse themselves. The system was new – the first workhouse was probably opened in Exeter in the 1650s – though the principle had been established towards the end of the reign of Elizabeth I; several were opened in London by 1700. And there was always a temptation, enshrined in law in 1662, to drive the poor – especially the migrant poor – into the next parish where they became someone else's responsibility.

John Keeling built this fire engine in 1678; it would have required continual refilling.

At a time of crisis, everyone would lend a hand to the pump, literally so in the frequent case of fire, but this was run on a parish basis and was not equal to the task of dealing with a major conflagration. During the four days of the Fire of London, in September 1666, the mayor attempted to co-ordinate fire-fighting, ordering that the houses in the path of the fire be torn down, but his efforts were overwhelmed by the heat of the flames and the strength of the wind. In the ensuing years the City acquired suitable equipment, but did not engage a force of fire-fighters. However, a private fire service was organised by Nicholas Barbon, the inventor of fire insurance, and his example was followed by others. A property owner put the mark of his insurer (firemark) on the outside of the house, and only the fire brigade run by that insurer would tackle the blaze.

Life in England's prisons was bearable only for those with sufficient resources to buy comfort and safety from bullying.

A reliable citizen might also be required to sit on a jury, and on one notable occasion in 1680 the judge, furious at the jury's refusal to convict two Quakers for illegal assembly, threw them all into prison for a week (eventually he had to back down, thereby creating the rule that a judge may not harass a jury).

Worse than being a juror, of course, was to be accused of a crime. Theft and burglary were very common, and anyone convicted of stealing goods worth more than a shilling from a private individual – or more than five shillings from a shop – could receive a death penalty; a lesser thief might get away with being branded on the cheek. A suspect might be apprehended by a parish constable or watchman, or by one of the privately operating thief-takers who could be hired by a victim to have someone brought to justice. The case was usually heard summarily by the judge, and an accused person's chances of acquittal were not good. The upshot might be prison, public humiliation (perhaps in the pillory or stocks) or death, normally by hanging. A pregnant woman could plead for a stay of execution, but prison was itself a ghastly punishment, only bearable for those who could afford to buy food and other services from the staff, or have them brought by friends. London alone had well over a hundred prisons. Some convicts might be deported to the Caribbean or American colonies, though in general these preferred to attract more reliable citizens to build their new society.

HEALTH

IN 1665, THE WORST VISITATION of the bubonic plague since the Black Death three hundred years earlier killed 100,000 Londoners in just a few summer months. Any house where the disease struck had its door nailed shut, its victims isolated inside with food brought to them and their neighbours warned to stay away by a red cross painted on the door with the words 'Lord have mercy on us'. Those who could, fled the city in panic (including the royal court and many doctors), but the Plague soon spread to other cities, such as Cambridge and York. Each night the dead were thrown onto carts and buried in great communal pits – which can still be seen in York – beyond the city walls. Though the Plague had a less severe impact in country areas where people lived in less crowded conditions, one village, Eyam in Derbyshire, became famous when a visit from a traveller led to an outbreak. The local rector realised that the disease could be contained only if the villagers remained where they were and refused any contact with the outside world. Four in five of them died, but the rest of the county was spared.

The bills of mortality, comprising detailed weekly reports of death, parish by parish, present a graphic picture of both the suffering caused by the Plague and other diseases, and the serious and innovative attempts made to collect hard data about their incidence.

Opposite:
Jan Steen's painting shows a doctor confidently taking the pulse of a wealthy woman.

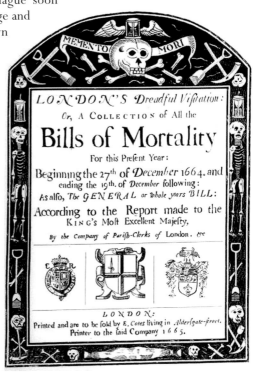

MEMENTO MORI

LONDON'S Dreadful Visitation:

Or, A COLLECTION of All the

Bills of Mortality

For this Present Year:

Beginning the 27ᵗʰ of *December* 1664. and ending the 19ᵗʰ. of December following:

As also, The *GENERAL* or *whole years* BILL:

According to the Report made to the KING's Most Excellent Majesty,

By the *Company of Parish-Clerks of* London. &c

LONDON:

Printed and are to be fold by E. *Cotes* living in *Alderfgate-fireet,* Printer to the faid Company 1 6 6 5.

In 1722, Daniel Defor wrote a fictional account of the Plague, entitled *Journal of the Plague Year*:

London might well be said to be all in tears; the mourners did not go about the streets indeed, for nobody put on black or made a formal mourning for their nearest friends; but the voice of the mourners was truly heard in the streets. The shrieks of women and children at the windows and doors of their houses where their nearest relatives were perhaps dying or just dead, were so frequent to be heard as we passed the streets that it was enough to pierce the stoutest heart in the world to hear them. Towards the latter end [of the visitation] men's hearts were hardened, and death was so always before their eyes, that they did not so much concern themselves for the loss of their friends, expecting that themselves should be summoned the next hour.

The Plague had ravaged Holland a couple of years earlier, but could not be kept from crossing the Channel, despite the two countries being at war. It was probably spread by the fleas of black rats. This was, however, not understood, and some thought that dogs and cats carried the disease, so that tens of thousands of these animals were killed, inadvertently increasing the rat population.

There was no cure. The illness began with sneezing, and large painful swellings developed in the lymph nodes in the armpits and groin; called buboes, these led to death a few days later. Others

The Plague emptied London's streets of any but those carrying corpses off for burial.

Eyam, in Derbyshire, is still renowned as the village that chose to sacrifice itself for the benefit of the rest of the county, by declaring a self-imposed quarantine as soon as the Plague arrived.

believed the disease was a result of a miasma, or bad air, and people wore bizarre masks or carried nosegays of herbs — but to no effect. Medical knowledge was still, for the most part, based on the 1,500-year-old theory of the four humours, and despite a growing interest in scientific investigation, the medical profession was slow to engage in innovative research into the causes of disease or its treatment.

'Plague doctors' sometimes wore bizarre masks with beaks filled with herbs to keep the noxious 'miasma' away.

Many quacks and 'wise women' advertised their services in the almanacs. Their treatments were mainly of little value; but even the highly educated physicians, with degrees from Oxbridge, Leiden or Padua, relied on bizarre pills and potions, and on frequent purging, vomiting and bleeding. Apothecaries frequently distrusted the physicians, and promoted their own remedies which they sold over the counter, but they did engage in a serious study of the healing power of plants, founding a garden (now known as the Physic Garden) in Chelsea in 1673 for the training of apprentices and study of non-native plants. Chirurgeons or surgeons performed gruesome operations with minimal anaesthetics but with occasional success: Pepys survived an operation for kidney stones and celebrated the anniversary each year thereafter. John Evelyn's brother, though, died of the same operation.

It is not surprising that people resorted, wherever possible, to self-help manuals. They always

The Worshipful Company of Apothecaries set up its garden in Chelsea to teach apprentices. Its coat of arms, still over the gate, shows a golden youthful Apollo, god of healing, astride the serpent disease.

did what they could to avoid hospitals, as these were only for the poor and the care they received was variable at best. St Bartholomew's and St Thomas's in London did what they could with a handful of medical staff and three hundred beds. In the closing years of the century the Royal Naval Hospital was created at Greenwich, and built by Christopher Wren over the coming decades for seamen and their families. Bedlam in south London was the country's only public mental hospital, and it was treated as much as an opportunity for sightseeing as for treatment of its sixty-odd 'lunatick and distracted' patients. There were other such institutions run privately: some, it was said, to take wives men no longer wanted.

Childbirth was inevitably one of the most dangerous moments in the life of both mother and child, and the birth would be attended by a group of 'gossips' – friends and relatives who were supposed to support the mother, and a midwife, who might be licensed but whose knowledge was primarily based on tradition, hearsay and – some thought – witchcraft. Some (male) surgeons attempted to deal with complications but had to argue with the midwives to be allowed access, a situation described by Elizabeth Freke in 1675, who was told by a surgeon that her unborn child was already dead and had to be removed from her womb:

> Whilst the man-midwife was putting on his butcher's habit to come about me, my great and good God that never failed me raised me up a good woman midwife who … for about two or three hours in her shift worked till … I was safely delivered.

Painful death from puerperal fever – now known to result from infection introduced by surgeon or midwife – was not an uncommon fate: almost two per cent of births resulted in the death of the mother.

Dentistry was another almost inescapable trial. The rise in sugar consumption meant that dental health, which had been relatively good in previous centuries, was beginning to deteriorate and some people tried to keep their teeth clean by scraping away plaque or rinsing the mouth with lemon juice. Mild pain was treated with cloves or tobacco, but an infected tooth had to be pulled – something done with the assistance of a large pair of pliers. Some people had a set of false teeth made of either ivory or of the teeth of the dead, and held in place by wires.

Smallpox was common, and a highly contagious disease: it was so prevalent among children in towns that much of the surviving adult populace was immune, though migrants from the countryside might still succumb. Recovery occurred in half of all cases, though it might leave unsightly pock-marks. By the end of the century, a few people were undergoing inoculation: deliberate infection with the disease in a manner that was unlikely to cause severe illness but likely to give immunity from future outbreaks.

Poor eyesight could be treated with spectacles, and the ability of people to read the small, densely printed books and newspapers of the day by candlelight is remarkable. Other common ailments included sexually transmitted diseases – mercury was a common, but toxic, treatment for syphilis – and gout, brought on by overindulgence in a rich diet.

Despite the best efforts of the medical men, death was omnipresent, and like everything else became an occasion to turn a profit. The first undertakers opened up shop in 1673, and in the succeeding years many such touted for business with advertisements and trade cards graphically depicting the paraphernalia of death. People were supposed patriotically to buy shrouds of English wool at £5 each, though most preferred to have timber coffins as well. Immediately after death, the sexton was informed, who rang the bell of the local parish church. The corpse was cleaned and

Above right: The 'infallible mountebank, or quack-doctor' put on a show to convince passers-by of the benefits of his nostrum, according to this satirical print of the 1680s.

Right: This print shows a woman undergoing a mastectomy; survival rates are not recorded.

The Tomb of
Colonel Sir Philip
Frowde (d. 1674)
in Bath Abbey.

dressed for viewing by friends and family, though they might have to wait two weeks or more for the funeral and interment, with nothing but herbs and perhaps some embalming to allay the inevitable odours. The whole household would be draped in black, and the family would take it in turns to watch over the corpse. At the funeral, close friends of the deceased acted as pallbearers, as the cortège processed through the streets to the church. After the interment, the guests returned to the house for a 'drinking', and the reading of the will. People might remain in mourning for up to a year.

With almost everyone at least a nominal Christian, belief in the afterlife was practically universal. Though many people expressed, and undoubtedly felt, genuine sorrow at the loss of a family member, there was a broadly philosophical acceptance of the vicissitudes of life. Moralists, though, argued that disasters – like the Plague, or the Fire – were signs of God's displeasure (what was called 'divine retribution') for the nation's immorality and wickedness.

Although most people were placed in unmarked graves, funerary monuments for the wealthy might be placed inside churches. These recorded little more than the bare facts of life, profession, family and death, without sentiment but in serene confidence of the eternal life to come. Typical is this inscription in Folkestone parish church:

Here rest in The Lord, John PRAGELL Esq. 4 Times Mayor of this Towne, 16 Yeares Lieut. of his Majestie's Castle of Sand Gate in The Liberty of this Corporation, who died in his Mayoralty, Nov. 1 1676. Aged 73 yeares, a Batchelor, and left behind him only One Brother Mr Clement PRAGELL, Jurate, his Heire; who in his pious Remembrance erected This Tombe. Underneath This Stone/ entombed doth lye/The Representer of Majestie./Death is impartial, a bold Sargeant He,/T'arrest a Port's man in his Mayoralty./A Magistrate upright, and truly just,/Once here a Ruler; Alass, now turnd to Dust./But, here is his Glory; it is but a Remove/From this frail Earth, to be enthroned above.

Whatever their station in life, people all over England would have recognised its sentiments.

PLACES TO VISIT

NATIONAL TRUST PROPERTIES

For National Trust properties go to www.nationaltrust.org.uk and
navigate to the individual property.

Belton House, Grantham, Lincolnshire NG32 2LS.
  A large country house built in the 1680s by Sir John Brownlow.
Felbrigg Hall, Felbrigg, Norwich, Norfolk NR11 8PR.
  A fine seventeenth-century house with Georgian additions.
Ham House, Ham, Richmond, London, TW10 7RS.
  A fine Restoration-period property belonging to one of Charles
  II's most trusted minister, with much period detail.
Wallington, Cambo, Morpeth, Northumberland NE61 4AR.
  A country house built in 1688 around an old pele tower, and
  remodelled further in the eighteenth century.

OTHERS

Eyam Museum, Hawkhill Road, Eyam, Derbyshire S32, 5QL.
  www.eyammuseum.demon.co.uk
  The museum of the plague village, with many of its seventeenth-
  century houses well preserved.
Royal Hospital Chelsea, Royal Hospital Road, London, SW3 4SR.
  www.chelsea-pensioners.co.uk/home
  The Royal Hospital was founded in 1682 and built by Wren.
Old Royal Naval College, Greenwich, Greenwich, SE10 9LW.
  www.oldroyalnavalcollege.org
  Founded in 1694, the Hospital was, like its counterpart in
  Chelsea, planned by Wren, though also contributed to by others.
Hampton Court Palace, East Molesey, Surrey KT8 9AU.
  www.hrp.org.uk/hamptoncourtpalace/
  Hampton Court's extension in the 1690s by William III was
  intended to rival Versailles.
Ashmolean Museum, Beaumont Street, Oxford, UK, OX1 2PH.
  www.ashmolean.org
  Now housed in a more modern building, the Ashmolean is built
  on a founding collection established in the Restoration period.
Palace of Holyroodhouse, Canongate, The Royal Mile, EH8 8DX.
  www.royalcollection.org.uk
  This ancient Scottish palace contains an extension built for Charles
  II, although he never ventured into his northern kingdom.

INDEX

Page numbers in italic refer to illustrations